WORKBOOK

FOR

When You Pray

Bible Study Book with Video Access: A Study of Six Prayers in the Bible

Gerard Adams

This Book Belongs To

_____

_____

INTRODUCTION

This workbook is intended to guide and enrich your prayer quest.

Prayer is the universal language that unites humanity with God across time and culture. It is a sacred practice that allows us to pour our hearts out, seek guidance, find solace, and experience God's presence in our lives. This workbook delves into the intimate prayers of six key figures in the Bible and discovers the profound lessons they teach us about fellowship with God.

This workbook invites you to delve into the depths of Scripture by focusing on specific prayers and their context.

From the heartfelt cry of David in the Psalms to the intercession of Jesus and the Apostle Paul, we explore a variety of prayers that express joy, fear, devotion, thanksgiving and supplication. Through thought-provoking questions, reflective exercises, and interactive activities, this workbook provides a space for personal reflection, allowing you to apply the timeless principles of prayer to your own life and circumstances.

Remember, this workbook is not just an intellectual exercise, it is a spiritual pilgrimage. It is an invitation to meet the living God, to seek His wisdom, and to align our hearts with His will. The insights and revelations you gain from studying these six prayers in the Bible will awaken your passion for prayer and empower you to walk in a more intimate relationship with your Heavenly Father.

30 Days Scriptures on Prayers

James 5:16	1 Thessalonians 5:17
Psalm 5:3	Matthew 26:41
Matthew 6:9-13	Psalm 145:18
Philippians 4:6-7	Jeremiah 33:3
Matthew 21:22	John 14:13-14
Mark 11:24	Luke 11:9
John 14:13-14	Ephesians 6:18
Romans 8:26	Colossians 4:2
1 Timothy 2:8	Psalm 102:17
Hebrews 4:16	Psalm 145:18
1 Peter 5:7	Proverbs 15:29
Psalm 66:17	Isaiah 65:24
Luke 6:28	Matthew 7:7-8
1 John 5:14	Psalm 4:1
Colossians 4:2	Jeremiah 29:12

Reflect on your understanding of prayer.
How would you, in your own words, define
prayer? How does it affect your life?

_____

_____

_____

_____

_____

_____

_____

How has your prayer life been?

_____

_____

_____

_____

_____

_____

_____

_____

_____

Do you find it difficult to pray? Why?

_____

_____

_____

_____

_____

_____

_____

Do you find it difficult to think of words to say
to God when you pray?

_____

_____

_____

_____

_____

_____

_____

_____

Are you worried that some feelings are too strong to express to God?

_____

_____

_____

_____

_____

Do you think God hears your prayer?

_____

_____

_____

_____

_____

_____

_____

_____

Do you think you are praying
the right way?

_____

_____

_____

_____

_____

_____

Write down the order in which you pray

_____

_____

_____

_____

_____

_____

_____

Reflect on the line "Our Father, who art in heaven." What does this phrase mean to you personally? How does it shape your understanding of God and your relationship with Him?

_____

_____

_____

_____

_____

_____

Consider the line "Hallowed be Thy name." What does it mean to honor and revere God's name? How can you actively live out this aspect of the Lord's Prayer in your daily life?

_____

_____

_____

_____

_____

_____

Meditate on the phrase "Thy kingdom come, Thy will be done on earth as it is in heaven." What does it mean to seek God's kingdom and align your will with His? How can you actively work towards bringing His kingdom values into your community?

_____

_____

_____

_____

_____

_____

Contemplate the line "Give us this day our daily bread." How does this request for daily sustenance connect to your reliance on God's provision? How can you cultivate a sense of gratitude and trust in God's faithfulness through this aspect of the prayer?

_____

_____

_____

_____

_____

_____

Reflect on the phrase "Forgive us our trespasses as we forgive those who trespass against us." How does this statement challenge you to examine your own heart and extend forgiveness to others? What steps can you take to foster a spirit of forgiveness in your relationships?

_____

_____

_____

_____

_____

_____

_____

Consider the line "Lead us not into temptation, but deliver us from evil." How does this plea for guidance and protection shape your understanding of spiritual warfare and the need for God's help in navigating challenges? How can you actively seek His guidance and strength in the face of temptation?

Meditate on the phrase "For Thine is the kingdom, and the power, and the glory forever." What does it mean to acknowledge and surrender to God's ultimate authority and glory? How can you cultivate a posture of surrender and worship in your own life?

_____

_____

_____

_____

_____

_____

Reflect on the line "And forgive us our debts, as we also have forgiven our debtors." How does this statement emphasize the importance of extending grace and mercy to others? How can you actively practice forgiveness and reconciliation in your relationships?

_____

_____

_____

_____

_____

_____

_____

Consider the phrase "Give us this day our daily bread." How does this statement invite you to cultivate a sense of dependence on God for your physical and spiritual needs? How can you actively seek His provision and sustenance in your life?

_____

_____

_____

_____

_____

_____

Meditate on the line "Thy will be done on earth as it is in heaven." What does it mean to align your desires and actions with God's perfect will? How can you actively seek to fulfill God's purposes and bring about His will in your sphere of influence?

_____

_____

_____

_____

_____

_____

Write down ways you can approach God in prayer when presenting your requests or petitions to Him?

_____

_____

_____

_____

_____

_____

_____

What should be the attitude of your heart when you bring your specific needs and desires before God in prayer?

_____

_____

_____

_____

_____

_____

_____

How can you align your petitions with God's will and seek His guidance and wisdom in your requests?

_____

_____

_____

_____

_____

_____

Write down the specific principles or guidelines you should follow when presenting your requests to God in prayer?

_____

_____

_____

_____

_____

_____

Write down the ways you can cultivate patience and trust in God's timing when waiting for answers to your prayers of petition

_____

_____

_____

_____

_____

_____

Psalm 139 acknowledges God's intimate knowledge and understanding of us. How does understanding this deep connection influence the way you approach praise as a form of prayer?

_____

_____

_____

_____

_____

_____

List the benefits of praising God according to Psalm 139

_____

_____

_____

_____

_____

_____

_____

Write down ways incorporating praise into your prayers help you express gratitude for God's continual presence and seek His guidance in every aspect of your life?

_____

_____

_____

_____

_____

_____

_____

How does Psalm 13's expression of lament in prayer resonate with your own personal experiences of hardship or struggle?

_____

_____

_____

_____

_____

_____

In what ways do you find solace or comfort in the act of offering a prayer of lament, similar to the psalmist's plea for God's attention and intervention?

_____

_____

_____

_____

_____

_____

_____

_____

Reflecting on Psalm 13, how do you navigate the tension between expressing your honest emotions and maintaining faith and trust in God during times of distress or unanswered prayers?

_____

_____

_____

_____

_____

_____

Have you ever experienced a transformation or deepening of your relationship with God through the process of engaging in prayers of lament, as the psalmist did? If so, can you describe that experience?

_____

_____

_____

_____

_____

_____

How do you incorporate the language and themes of lament from Psalm 13 into your personal prayer life, and what impact does it have on your spiritual journey and growth?

_____

_____

_____

_____

_____

_____

_____

How does Paul's example of offering intercessory prayers for others inspire you to prioritize the needs and well-being of those around you in your own prayer life?

_____

_____

_____

_____

_____

_____

Write down the names of a few people you want to pray for and say a prayer for them

---

In what ways have you seen the power of intercessory prayer manifest in the lives of those you have prayed for, similar to Paul's experiences of seeing God's transformative work in the lives of the early Christians?

_____

_____

_____

_____

_____

_____

In what ways have you seen the power of intercessory prayer manifest in the lives of those you have prayed for?

_____

_____

_____

_____

_____

_____

How do you discern the specific needs and concerns of others in order to offer effective and targeted intercessory prayers?

_____

_____

_____

_____

_____

_____

_____

How has engaging in intercessory prayer, following the pattern set by Paul, shaped your own heart and mindset towards others, cultivating compassion, empathy, and a deeper sense of interconnectedness within the body of Christ?

_____

_____

_____

_____

_____

_____

_____

How do you understand the concept of oneness with God and others in light of Jesus' teachings on prayer and unity, and how does this understanding impact your own spiritual journey?

_____

_____

_____

_____

_____

_____

_____

Prayer is the key

Made in the USA
Las Vegas, NV
03 December 2024

13313782R00026